THE PROCESS

THE PROCESS

An Engaging Program That Explores Why You Behave
the Way You Do and What You Can Do About It

Tom Steward

Library of Congress Control Number: 2022913702
ISBN: Hardcover   978-1-6698-3929-3
               Softcover   978-1-6698-3928-6
               eBook   978-1-6698-3927-9

Scripture quotations marked NASB are taken from the New American Standard
Bible®, Copyright © 1960, 1962, 1963, 1968, 1971, 1972, 1973, 1975, 1977,
1995 by The Lockman Foundation. Used by permission.

Print information available on the last page.

Rev. date: 07/26/2022

To order additional copies of this book, contact:
Xlibris
844-714-8691
www.Xlibris.com
Orders@Xlibris.com
843419

CONTENTS

This book is a manual that describes
a supportive, encouraging, and nonjudgmental healing program
for individuals who are at unease with their alcohol use
(or any substance or behavior)
and also for those who want to help them,
who hope to find the true source behind their behavior,
in a way that results in freedom and empowerment.

For
The Curious
Who Asks Why
And What

To all my friends and loved ones
Anyone . . . You
Who drink somewhat casually, routinely, or a whole lot more
Or are dependent on another substance
Or have engaged in any untoward behavior
Hurting or concerning others, even loved ones
Or perhaps have made a big mess of your life
And you tell yourself repeatedly that you need to stop this
Yet you do it again, repeating the behavior you don't want
Leaving you empty and ashamed and powerless
You wish you could stop, but you don't, or can't
And you ask so very often, "Why do I do this?"

Restoration

In the Babemba tribe of South Africa, when a person acts irresponsibly or unjustly, he is placed in the center of the village, alone and unfettered. All work ceases, and every man, woman, and child in the village gathers in a large circle around the accused individual. Then each person in the tribe speaks to the accused, one at a time, each recalling the good things the person in the center of the circle has done in his lifetime. Every incident, every experience that can be recalled with any detail and accuracy, is recounted. All his positive attributes, good deeds, strengths, and acts of kindness are recited carefully and at length. This tribal ceremony often lasts for several days.

In the end, the tribal circle is broken, a joyous celebration takes place, and the person is symbolically and literally welcomed back into the tribe.

This story teaches us a lot about the wisdom of simple people. In our increasingly fast-paced and sophisticated world, we have forgotten to forgive and we have forgotten that without forgiveness it is difficult for someone to achieve the peace of mind that we all long for.

Many times, someone's bad deed erases in our minds all the good things he or she has done. Disappointed with someone's behavior at some point, we tend to forget that a person can not be reduced only to a mistake or injustice he or she committed. We have to see the person in the light of all the deeds that define him, many of these being good deeds.

—Jack Kornfield

When a person has done something, behaved in a certain way that is not consistent with their true nature, restoration is needed. This is to be done with utmost tender graciousness and gentle kindness so that the recipient may be reminded of their true worth and value.

This is the intention—to restore the one to true self, the radiance of who they really are in the broader dimensions.

The community gathers to impress upon the one, with words of fond reminiscence of brighter moments, to remember their divine nature, *imago Dei* and uncarved block. Once this is achieved and the person takes to heart this sacred message, there will be a shift in consciousness, a propelling forward, and a newfound resolve to carry on.

Preface

*The great fact is just this, and nothing less: That we have
had deep and effective spiritual experiences which have
revolutionized our whole attitude toward life, toward our
fellows and towards God's universe. The central fact of our lives
today is the absolute certainty that our Creator has entered into
our hearts and lives in a way which is indeed miraculous.*
—The Big Book of AA

So you drink. Yet how much? And is your level of drinking a problem? You must be bothered by it to some degree because you are here, reading this.

How do you know if you have a drinking problem? Are you addicted? Is it an addiction to alcohol? And what about that term *alcoholic*? Are you an alcoholic? Or are you an abusive drinker with an overdependency?

These are just words to describe behavior, yet do you turn to alcohol more than necessary? Are you a casual drinker or periodic? Can you put alcohol down anytime you want to? Do others tell you that you drink too much?

Amen Clinics have presented twelve warning signs that you have a drinking problem.[1] Here they are:

1. You have more drinks than planned.
2. Alcohol plays a featured role in your life, and you spend a lot of time thinking about drinking, obtaining alcohol, or recovering from drinking.
3. The day after drinking, you feel bad and experience brain fog, irritability, tiredness, or low motivation.
4. It's causing problems in your relationships.
5. You're getting into trouble at work, school, with money, and/or the law.
6. You get sick physically and/or psychologically.
7. You withdraw from life and from hobbies you normally enjoy.
8. You take dangerous risks while drinking that could harm you or others.
9. When you drink, your behavior is out of character, and you say or do things that make you feel ashamed, guilty, and remorseful.
10. You've developed a tolerance and need more alcohol to get the same effect.
11. You've tried unsuccessfully to reduce your drinking.
12. You keep drinking despite negative consequences.

And then there is the CAGE questionnaire, developed by Dr. John Ewing, founding director of the Bowles Center for Alcohol Studies at

---

[1]   https://www.amenclinics.com/blog/how-do-you-know-if-you-have-an-alcohol-problem/?trk_msg=25ITCK7SV5D495I8BA52M8U21G&trk_contact=JS86R14IGTOOO2M6OL9RQN04V0&trk_sid=CFLD NRQDQ2NNHN5EVHH2PC0B4K&trk_link=C54EDSHNR 7Q4PFNCVA8FB79TOS&utm_source=ACI-Listrak&utm_medium=Email&utm_term=Read+More&utm_campaign=Friday+Send

the University of North Carolina.[2] CAGE is a widely used assessment for identifying drinking issues.

Here are the CAGE questions:

- **C:** Have you ever felt you should **c**ut down on your drinking?
- **A:** Have people **a**nnoyed you by criticizing your drinking?
- **G:** Have you ever felt bad or **g**uilty about your drinking?
- **E:** Have you ever had a drink first thing in the morning to steady your nerves or to get rid of a hangover (**e**ye-opener)?

A score of 2 or more is significant, and the higher the score, the higher the risk of complications. Wherever you are on this scale, and if you are willing, what is contained in these pages is a program for you.

In this manual, there are seven modules, which are described below:

Module 1: *Transparency*
Looking honestly at yourself and who you really are.

Module II: *The Life You Now Live*
Considering what has become of you and how drinking has impacted your life.

Module III: *Sorrows That Carve Deep*
Processing the pain and trauma of your life to experience healing.

Module IV: *Relationship Repair*
Examining your relationships to begin the process of repair.

---

[2] https://www.hopkinsmedicine.org/johns_hopkins_healthcare/downloads/all_plans/CAGE%20Substance%20Screening%20Tool.pdf.

Module V: *Forgiveness and Amends*
Assessing the need to forgive and be forgiven.

Module VI: *Transcendence*
Seeing how your progress has led you to your
awakening.

Module VII: *A New Life*
Observing a new reality as you live a life of freedom
and triumph.

I have written this manual because I have heard too many stories of
those who feel that they drink too much and would like to stop or
curtail their drinking. These individuals do not like what drinking
has done to them and their lives, which includes the impact of
drinking on their social life and physical health.

There are others who have had serious health challenges related
to alcohol consumption, and some have even died. I hope we can
gather in community for support and encouragement to save lives
and restore relationships.

As I wrote this manual, it suddenly dawned on me that the principles
in each module could be applied to any behavior or issue. No matter
what behavior you are concerned about, this writing can help.

It could be an overdependency, or what is often referred to as an
addiction, to drugs, sex, food, relationships, shopping, gambling,
anxiety, OCD, chocolate, anger/rage, and sugar, to name a few.
The list is endless, so insert your behavior of choice or even
obsession.

This program is called *The Process* because it is just that, a process. The focus will be precisely where you are, with acceptance and understanding, as you move forward step by step.

The journey is the destination, and the journey of a thousand miles begins with one step, to quote familiar phrases. And now, let's begin, at the beginning.

The Beginning

That Is Not Who You Are . . . This Is Who You Are

*Go slowly . . . Consent to it . . . But don't wallow in it . . . Know it
as a place of germination . . . And growth . . . Remember the light . . .
Take an outstretched hand if you find one . . . Exercise unused senses . . .
Find the path by walking it . . . Practice trust . . . Watch for dawn.*
—Marilyn Chandler McEntyre, "What to Do in the Darkness"

Welcome

You have made the decision to go through this process, and for that, I applaud you. You must want to grow and change in some way. It takes courage to do that, so I would like to honor you up front for that choice.

You must be contending in some way with a substance, most likely alcohol. It could be a drug, prescription or not. You may also be associated with someone who is struggling with a substance, and you would like to support them. The behavior in question for you could be something else altogether.

Know at the onset here that you can be at any level of drinking to be on this course. This program is for you if you have a serious drinking problem, a moderate one, or you are not drinking at all. You may be using another substance, like any drug or food or a particular behavior.

Truthfully, there are tools in this program that will help anyone. There are those who are taking part in this program who have been involved in unhealthy and abusive relationships. Some are isolating certain behaviors that present issues for them.

I have been a casual and not-so-casual drinker for decades. I love gin, yet I have also imbibed in beer and wine a lot.

On many occasions, the people around me say it has been a problem because I have behaved in ways I do not while sober. I get moody or quiet, and I have spoken in a way that is mean or condescending. I have blacked out, not remembering what happened the night before.

My drinking has disturbed me for years, because I wanted to quit but have not been able to. Mostly, it bothered me because, in my quest to progress as a spiritual being, alcohol seemed to hinder this objective.

Something happened on April 6, 2022, and my relationship with alcohol significantly changed. I hardly drink at all anymore, and when I do, it is not a problem.

I also lost a son to a drug overdose on December 15, 2012. I went to his house only to find him lifeless after he used substances the night before. He was a beautiful soul, and I miss him greatly. I wrote about him and what happened in the book *Holy Pride and Love of Self.*

I would say that my strength and resolve to change my relationship with alcohol did not come from feeling bad about all the negative consequences of drinking. No, I wasn't motivated to stop by shame or even fear.

My drinking changed because I came to realize who I am as a spiritual being on a quest for wholeness. I also experienced healing that enabled me to remove the emotional conditions behind my drinking. This course will guide you through a similar process, yet tailored to you and your unique life.

Questions to Ponder

As we begin, we are not going to focus on all the so-called bad aspects of your life. I would like you to consider the good aspects of your life. You may be representing yourself in a certain way in your life that is not who you are. It is my aim at the onset to direct you toward who you really are, your true self.

First, I am curious about your finer attributes. What are your strengths, skills, and abilities? What do you hear from others when they say nice things about you? Go ahead and write these down here in the space below or on another sheet of paper.

Now, I would like to know about your greatest accomplishments. What are your finest achievements? What have you done in your life that you are most proud of? Write these successes down too.

Okay, very good. I would also like to know what problem or obstacle you have been able to overcome in your life. Write about a time when you had the grit and determination and insight to solve something for yourself or another person or in a particular situation that enabled you to come out the victor. Write your answer in the space provided.

Excellent! Now, I would like to ask that you provide three words that best describe you. The only rule is that these words must be positive. No negativity or put-downs here. I would like you to present three very specific words that best capture the essence of who you really are. Write these down in the space below.

Finally, I am going to ask that you use your imagination for a moment. I would like you to see yourself free from your struggle with the substance you use and, possibly, overuse. Envision yourself not struggling with any substance or even the behavior you have chosen.

What would your life be like if you did not represent this behavior? Who would you be if you were free from the shame and powerlessness of engaging in that action, which has caused so much trouble for you? Hold this image of you living in freedom in your mind as often as possible.

Focusing on What You Want, Not on What You Don't Want

The reason why I would like you to entertain this last question is that you likely have the tendency to focus on what you don't want. When there is a problem, you may too often fixate on it while hoping to overcome it. This dilemma then becomes a pervasive reality that you have trouble shaking.

If you are like most of us, you tend to be consumed with the negative rather than the positive, with your mistakes and failures rather than your potential and your triumphs, and with what happened that was wrong or bad rather than what is good or positive. Consequently, you will have a hard time overcoming anything when you are obsessing on it.

There is a saying that goes like this: "What you resist persists." You cannot resist or stop doing something when you are glaring at it. It will persist in your life because you are providing it with attention. So as we proceed, our predominant preoccupation will be on solutions, not problems.

Another favorite quote of mine is this: "You cannot solve a problem with the same consciousness that created it." As we proceed through this process, it will be important to rise above, to experience a greater consciousness, than the perspective that created the problem.

You will need to get above your problem and rise to a higher transcended perception to see more clearly from an aerial perspective. This will help a lot because you won't be able to solve your life dilemmas when you are in the consciousness or mindset equal to the problem.

What I have been able to overcome in my life was accomplished by focusing on what I wanted, not on what I didn't want. Many years ago, this phrase came to me: "You need to stop stopping." I knew I needed to stop this stopping business and begin the starting process of what I really wanted in my life. So I did, and have, as much as necessary.

Compassion, Not Judgment

Notice that during this writing, I have intentionally not used negative terminology to describe your behavior. This behavior, drinking or whatever, is often referred to as a sickness, an illness, or a disease.

Overuse of alcohol or substances is normally known as addiction, or an abusive or destructive tendency. There is also the use of the words "being an alcoholic" or "having alcoholism" or even "drug addict" and other words like that. I did call it a problem above, yet that was to offer you the selected quote.

I hope you can begin to see what you are doing in as neutral terms as possible. The reason is, shame is one of the energies that fuel overdrinking, and this shame needs to be used wisely. Shame by itself is a horrible motivator. You won't stop your drinking by feeling bad about it.

Begin to express kindness to yourself. Be nice! That will help a lot. Beating yourself up will not be helpful. You know that because that is very likely what you have been doing, and you are still drinking more than you would like or behaving in the way you would rather not.

Similarly, it will be beneficial to offer compassion, not judgment, to yourself and what is occurring in your life. Remember this motto: Compassion, Not Judgment.

Judging yourself will not produce what you want. You have done enough of that too, and it hasn't changed anything. You are really doing the best you can. You are trying, and you are here looking for something that will help you. And here we are together. Hooray!

Also, we are finding that trauma is associated with the overuse of substances. This is also true for any other stubborn behavior. People who are called addicts or addicted or alcoholics have been traumatized in one way or another. They are doing what they know to chase away the pain of years of abuse and disappointment and heartache.

These people (you and I) have been through a lot, and using a substance to ease the deep ache is the habitual tendency. This anguish is often beneath the level of awareness, yet it wreaks havoc in the user's life.

This may also be true for you. You have been through a lot. You have pain and anguish to some degree. All you want is for it to go away. Healing your suffering is essential as you begin to understand your motivations to engage in any behavior. In the meantime, offer kindness to yourself as we begin to unravel the mystery of why you do what you do.

Now take a few deep breaths to come into a calm space and begin to believe in yourself. Someone needs to believe in you, and I pick you. You can do this. You will do it. You will get to the other side of what is presenting these issues in your life.

We will do this together. Everything is going to be all right. And you will learn a lot. You will acquire new tools and skills and attitudes. There will be healing and transformation—yes, there will be. This will be what you need for the best version of you to emerge.

Reflection

Spend some time now on contemplating that image of you that you created earlier in this reading. This is a visual picture of you free from that behavior you can't seem to stop. It is a picture of you not feeling the heartache and pain that has become so ever-present in your life. Ponder this, and meditate on it often—and even now—in this moment.

Let it develop into an advanced version of who you really are—your higher self. This is the best self you can offer. Imagine, with wild abandon, what your life would be like if this true self were manifested every day of your life.

Who would you be? How would you be different? Get to know this person and allow it to become more ever-present in your life.

And know that this aspect of you is already a reality in you right now and is guiding you in your evolution. Yes, your true self is what is helping you along this path of recovery.

Take comfort in that, and offer gratitude to your new friend.

MODULE I

Transparency

Our spiritual journey requires a deepening awareness of our own shadow and light. It requires a rigorous commitment to "catching ourselves in the act" of automatic, programmed responses. It requires choosing instead to respond from the place of light in us and to call forth that light in every life we touch. It requires a descent into our deepest, truest self, into the wellspring of Divine Love in us. That descent involves a thousand deaths to the ego, a constant pattern of letting go and surrendering at deeper and deeper levels. The descent often involves suffering which we do not choose—it chooses us.
—K. Killian Noe, *Descent into Love: How Recovery Café Came to Be*

Entertaining a New You

All right, let's move on. Recall all your positive attributes we discussed in the previous section. Review them if you need to as often as you are able. Don't forget to believe in yourself. Hopefully, you are already doing that.

Additionally, remember to be kind to *yourself* as you proceed through this process. Compassion, Not Judgment is the new motto. Be nice to *yourself.*

Recall that vision of you representing your best self. I asked before what your life would be like if you were not engaged in that behavior (or thinking or feeling, etc.) that causes these concerns in your life.

Go into that visual and entertain it for a little longer now. Keep this goal ahead of you as often as you are able. What you resist persists, and what you focus on becomes your reality. Now choose what you would like to set before you as an image that will guide you.

> If you were not a drinker, or not a drinker that arouses so much trouble, what would that look like?
>
> What would it be like without the shame and regret and guilt for what you have done to make a mess of your life?
>
> Or if you have relationships that are troublesome, what if there were peace and harmony with others instead?
>
> What if you didn't live with the grief and pain and anguish and sorrow in response to the losses you have experienced?
>
> What would your life be like if you did not struggle emotionally with sadness or depression or anxiety?
>
> What would it be like if you did not engage in compulsive or obsessive behaviors?

What would you see in the various contexts of your life? How would you conduct yourself? How would you behave and interact with others? See this in as much detail as you are able. I have provided space for you to record what you would see in your life.

What thoughts would you have about yourself? What would you say about yourself? What would others say about you? Write down the words that would be said about you by you and others in the space below.

What would this feel like to you? What emotion would this new you register inside of you? Have you had that feeling before?

Where do you feel that feeling in your body? What is it like for you as you allow this to be strong? Can you make it even stronger?

To learn new behavior and integrate it into your life, first, you will need to see it to have an image imprinted in your visual memory.

Second, you will have new thoughts about it as you hear yourself in your own mind. Use words to describe these changes. You will also hear others make positive comments about the changes that are occurring.

Then third, you will feel differently, and these emotions will anchor this new experience into your body.

In short, behavior change includes seeing, hearing, and feeling the changes in your life. This is how you will transition into the new you that you have envisioned, created, and begun to manifest in your life.

Getting Real

I would like to now lead you into some honesty about you and your drinking. If you are currently not drinking, you can reference your past drinking behaviors. You can also answer the questions below, even if drinking is not the issue of your life.

This module is called "Transparency" because we are going to look at what is really going on. This may be painful, so draw the strength you have within as we proceed.

As we move into this section, try your best to minimize the shame about yourself and your life. That won't help you at all. You will feel some shame and guilt, yet observe this as much as you are able and pull away if you start to become overwhelmed.

You may be aware of the impact your drinking or particular behavior is having on your life, or there might be a certain measure of denial. You may have developed a thousand excuses for yourself. Or you may already be honest with yourself, at least a little.

Write in the space provided below or on another sheet of paper a detailed accounting of your drinking habits—what do you drink, how much do you drink, and when do you drink? If you are not a drinker, write about the pain or struggle in your life from your behavior.

Spend some time with this, because your honesty about yourself and your actions is essential in your recovery.

How is what you are doing or what is happening in your life causing you pain? How are you contributing to the problems and issues in your life?

How has your drinking or behavior affected others? How do others feel in response to what you are doing? Have you hurt anyone in any way? How?

How has your drinking or behavior impacted you? Has it put any aspect of your life in jeopardy? How does it keep you from being the person you want to be?

What is the biggest negative impact of your drinking or behavior, the worst thing that has happened? How have your actions hurt you the most?

All right, good job. How was that? What was it like for you to admit these things? Did you leave anything out? Were you brutally honest or did you provide vague generalizations? Whatever you did is just fine, for now.

Additionally, have you told anyone else these things? Do others know the extent of your drinking or behavior, or have you found a way to hide it?

Is it possible that you believe you have hidden your actions, but others really do know? If someone else knows, do you have someone in your life who is confronting you about it?

You may think this person is a nag and they annoy the hell out of you, but just know they are afraid. They love you enough to point out how what you are doing is impacting them, and they have become fearful, perhaps even resentful, toward you.

You may be minimizing the details of what you are doing. That's typical for those engaged in out-of-control behaviors. What I am asking is that you highlight what is happening and the consequences that have arisen. You are increasing your level of honesty and awareness. Good job!

It is also possible that you are the one who is judging yourself the most. You may be the person who is hardest on yourself. None of this helps, but it happens. Draw from deep within you and show a little kindness to yourself.

Answer the following questions and write your answers in the space provided.

How has drinking or what you are doing helped you? What have you concluded are the benefits of drinking or behaving the way you do? In what ways have you told yourself that doing what you are doing is supposed to help?

What are the emotions that you experience the most in your life? What are your feelings on any given day at any time? What do you fccl before, during, and after drinking, or when you engage in the behavior you are highlighting here?

Now, what are your typical thoughts? You may need to take some time with this, but begin to consider the main thoughts that run through your mind. This may be what is known as stinking thinking, or some version of a negative thought life.

If you could isolate the most predominant thought in your life that is the most troublesome for you, what would that be? What is the one thought you have about yourself that is harming you the most?

Regarding this thought you have discovered, how does it affect your perception and view of the world? How do you react or what happens when you believe that thought?

Is this thought true? Can you absolutely know if it's true? Why or why not?

Who would you be like if you didn't believe that thought? What would your life be like?

What would you like to believe instead? If you could replace that thought with another one that would be more helpful and beneficial to you and your life, what would that be?

If this new thought were sufficiently integrated into your life, what would that be like? How would you feel? Would you behave differently? If so, how? How would your perspective and attitude change? Would you view yourself and others and the world around you differently? Write about these things below.

Now, please return to the picture you developed earlier. Do the above questions you answered in this section change anything about this image? Are you able to see it in a different light? Does it provide a different perspective to this picture? Write about this here.

Transparency

What I am asking you to do here is to become transparent about how you behave, what you feel, and what your dominant thoughts are. How you live, the choices you have made, have consequences. You may have hurt others, and even hurt yourself, yet we are aiming to make corrections to improve your life.

I hope you have also seen how you have choices and how you can make positive changes in your life. The above questions are meant to bring about these changes.

One of the renderings from *Merriam-Webster* for the word *transparency* is "a picture viewed by light shining through it." Being transparent is shining a light on what is being viewed. It may be like entering a dark room and turning the light on. The room is now seen more clearly because the light is shining in and through it.

What needs to be reinforced here is that you are not the darkness or the dark room or what is in the room, no matter how messy it is. You are the light that is providing illumination so you can see.

You are the light, yet you may know mostly darkness. The light will help you; it's pointing you to what needs to change, and that is what you are doing.

Let's continue this discussion as we consider how you can move from powerlessness to power, in response to what you are seeing in this now lighted room that you call your life.

Module II

The Life You Now Live

As soon as we admitted the possible existence of a Creative Intelligence, a Spirit of the Universe underlying the totality of things, we began to be possessed of a new sense of power and direction, provided we took other simple steps. We found that God does not make too hard terms with those who seek (this Spirit). *To us, the Realm of Spirit is broad, roomy, all inclusive; never exclusive or forbidding to those who earnestly seek. It is open, we believe, to all.*

—*The Big Book of AA*

The Initial Steps

The first three steps of Alcoholics Anonymous are as follows (with some minor revisions):

1. I admitted I was powerless over alcohol—that my life had become unmanageable.
2. I came to believe that a power greater than me could restore me to sanity.
3. I decided to turn my will and my life over to the care of God, Source, or Spirit, as this Being is understood and known.

In the original statement for step 1, the first word is *we*. It has been said that to change this to *I* would have negative consequences. This is so because to begin this process requires the recognition of a group of supportive individuals who have joined you in this quest. In saying "we," you admit and agree that you are not alone.

I choose to represent the word *I*, yet do remember that we are in this together—you and I and so many others. An online group is offered as a part of this program, and you can contact me at tomstewardpa@gmail.com for more details.

Powerlessness to Power

There seems to be so much over which we are powerless. We try to control so much that we are unable to manage with even a small measure of success.

We can't stop drinking or drugging or overeating. We can't stop making fools of ourselves or upsetting and hurting others. We don't seem to measure up to the standards and demands of others and too often feel not good enough. We can't stop the conflict with the people we love and care about the most. We have trouble controlling emotions like anger and sadness and depression. Anxieties and fears and obsessions and compulsions just keep happening. And then, people die, or in some way leave us, and we can't shake the grief and sorrow from our losses. We can't perform well enough at work and are unable to get our bosses to value our performance. We can't seem to find any purpose or meaning to this life we have been given, and we move through each day aimlessly. We can't find any satisfaction in relationships, and they all just fall flat or end way too soon. And then, that despair and hopelessness creeps in all too often, which is terrifying.

You may wonder if you have lost your mind. Are you insane or mentally deficient? Is there some sort of huge malfunction in body or brain or soul?

All these concerns may not be true for you, but some of them might. If so, what can you do? What might help?

You're not insane, by the way. You have just met your match. In some way unique to you, in any of the above ways—you have become powerless.

There is good news. There is a power. This power is greater than you, and it has the momentum to return you to a mind that is healthy and sound. It has the ability to provide purpose to your life and restore your life to some sense of decency and value.

I appreciate that AA refers to this power as "a creative intelligence" and "Spirit of the Universe underlying the totality of things" in the "broad, roomy, all-inclusive . . . Realm of Spirit." In so doing, anyone can entertain this greater power. No particular religion or set of beliefs is required. It is simply a recognition that there is a mysterious and transcendent power not far away . . . it is near.

In this way, you do not need to believe in God, and you may have concluded long ago that this God business is a fable that conveniently fits into one of the many stories of mythology or even a religion of imperialism that asserts too much influence into people's lives. You may even have issues with the deity of organized religion and carry enough suspicion to make you cautious.

Even more, you may believe that any concept of an ascended being is you, your higher self. You are the *creative intelligence* offered above in perhaps many of the variations that are currently understood.

This is all just fine. All that is asked is that you acknowledge some version of *transcendent greatness* around you and in you.

And then there is the action of surrendering to this power, a yielding to this Spirit or Creator or Source or you. It is here that you turn your will and your life over to the formidable sway of this tremendously potent force. This is achieved in whatever way you have come to experience this being or non-being or essence.

When you realize there is something you cannot do, it becomes apparent how much you are able to do. When you admit your powerlessness, a power begins to surge in and through you. When you believe with all your being that this power can help, that it can restore you, it surely does.

You suddenly become aware that this power greater than you is resident in you, captivating your entire being in awe-inspiring thrust. The Spirit of the universe and universes reside within your very soul, enabling your spirit to come alive. It is your true nature as one made in the image of the Divine.

This is your true self, who you really are. This recognition of something that was concluded to be outside and far away is intimately acquainted in the center of your being, representing your inherent divinity.

This is the Source—source consciousness, creator, higher mind, the ultimate, and all that is—that you surrender to. You turn your life and will over to this perennial power, or "primordial tower," as Rilke has written.

And why wouldn't you? How could you not? This is the perpetual essential action that introduces and reintroduces you to your sacred interior—that place within you that radiates beauty.

This is the path that you will take on this course. Don't be concerned that what was offered above seems foreign to you. We will journey together, and you will gain power that you have not known and did not believe was possible to attain.

Vital Spiritual Experience

There are two very important aspects of a recovery program. The first is overcoming hurts and wounds and trauma through healing and renewal. We will spend much time looking at your life, so you will experience the transformation that you long for.

The other aspect of this recovery program is a profound spiritual experience. *The Big Book* talks about apprehending a "vital spiritual experience." This is encountering God as you know God. You then surrender and move into the ineffable rhythms of divinity in whatever way it is known.

This spiritual experience cannot be planned or scheduled, yet there are certain actions that ensure its unveiling. It is an essential aspect of this program, and we will set the stage for its timely arrival and unveiling.

In this module, we will continue to address what you have done that has caused pain to yourself and others. In short, how you have hurt others.

In Module III, we will consider the pain of your life. This encompasses how others have hurt you.

In Module IV, we will focus on repairing your relationships. Your use of alcohol or any other substance or any behavior undoubtedly has had a harmful impact on your relationships. We will address this and find ways to bring some level of resolution to you and those you interact.

In Module V, we will engage the process of a moral inventory to make amends and offer forgiveness. Forgiveness is so important, yet it must be performed wisely and with a delicate touch.

Module VI and VII, transcendence and a new life, will be a lovely conclusion of this process. This is where everything will begin to come together as a culmination of all the hard work that has been achieved.

Believing in Power

Let's take some action. Please answer these questions in the space provided:

In what ways (be specific and thorough) has your life become unmanageable?

Does it feel to you like you have lost your mind to a certain degree and that there is something askew about your mental perceptions or the way you view yourself, others, and the world around you? Are there times when you feel even a little bit insane? Explain this, please, here.

How is your life out of control? Have you come to the place where you have concluded you are powerless over alcohol or any other substance or behavior? Why or why not?

How would you describe this so-called power greater than you? Please tell of the times when you have made contact.

In what ways have you turned your will and life over to this power? Explain this and provide as much detail as you can.

Describe how you have had a vital spiritual experience to any degree or measure. How has this benefitted you? If you have not had one of these spiritual experiences, how do you imagine what that would be like?

Creating a New Reality

I would like to present to you something I was introduced a few years ago from Dr. Joe Dispenza. I learned to strengthen my meditation practice with Dr. Joe and to also manifest my greatest desires from a place of infinite possibility.

There is a place of unlimited dimension and scope called the unified field. This is an endless field that is, somehow, expanding. Everything is there, including but not limited to *infinite possibilities*. (Ha!) All the resources you could ever want or desire that would enable you to live your best life are present in this field.

To manifest from this realm, there are three factors to consider:

1. Intention
2. Elevated emotion
3. Manifestation

These three points roughly correlate with Dr. Joe's teaching and are the way I have synthesized them for the benefit of myself and others.

For the sake of redundancy, recall the visual I keep reminding you. You know, the one where you are not drinking, or in any way not doing that thing that has turned your life into a personal domain of chaos and trouble and frustration. It's the image of you living out your best life. You are well, healthy, vibrant, and alive in the best and fullest sense. You are, in short, your true self.

Intention. If you were to apply an intention statement to that picture, what would it be? This is a short positive statement, grounded in the present moment, as if it were occurring now.

It could be something like "I am living a radiant life of abundance and free of any dependence on alcohol," or "I am healthy and well in every area of my life," or "my relationships are healthy, nurturing, and nourishing, and meet all of my needs." These are examples, yet I am asking that you develop your own and write it down in the space provided here.

Consider for a moment that your statement is true and is being carried out in your life in precisely the way you have envisioned. The picture you have chosen captures your intention and is a living testament to your greatest desires being realized. Bring this reality into the present moment, right now, and experience it as if it were really happening.

Elevated emotion. In your expanded imagination, as you see this intention in the current moment, what would this feel like? You have a visual, the intention, and you are pondering what it would feel like for that emotion to be registered in you in this moment.

What would this emotion be? Do you feel it now? Where do you feel it in your body? Pause for a moment and let it be real—*really real.* Let this emotion move deep in you and even become stronger. Write about this emotional experience here.

The intention has been created, and the corresponding emotion has been brought into the present moment to feel right now. When your entire consciousness and being registers this potential in this way, it concludes it is already occurring. It is just a matter of time for your creation to become a reality being manifested in your life.

Manifestation. You must see it, allowing the visual to be very strong, while locking the emotional experience in you as if it were already occurring. Dr. Joe calls this "living as if your prayers are already answered." You have apprehended that elevated emotion to such a degree that you are feeling it into your life.

This intention is of you living free, not living the life that has been so painful for you. You are seeing something else—a life of peace and fulfillment in whatever way you envision this.

In summary for this exercise, you have taken your picture and applied an intention statement to it. You allowed an elevated emotion to be associated with this potential event in a way that encapsulates what you are desiring.

You feel this emotion in the present moment, dragging it from a perceived future place of possibility into the now time, feeling it as if it were currently happening for you. The emotion is the key, and feeling it very deeply provides a signal to the wider part of you that you have a longing that you know unwaveringly will be delivered to you.

You then rehearse this, perhaps repeatedly, as often as you need to as you integrate it into your yielded consciousness. Your entire being now lines up with this predicted outcome, such that it cannot help but be dispensed to your life.

Making a Decision

The primary tenets of this module are described in the first three steps of the AA program. Know that this is no short course, and much work is involved.

I would encourage you to return to these ideas and practices in this section over and over. Take the following precepts with you as you move along this path and return to them as often as you need to.

A summary of the first three steps are listed here:

1. You (along with your new tribe) are powerless, and your life has become unmanageable.
2. There is a power greater than you that can restore you.
3. You now decide to turn your life and will over to this power in the way you conceive and understand it.

Next, we will consider the wounds and traumas of your life. It is possible that these hurts are the fuel that ignites your overdrinking or the behavior that is most troubling for you. Apprehending healing in key areas has the potential to remove the ignition switch that results in your powerless behavior.

Module III

The Sorrows That Carve Deep

The deeper that sorrow carves into your being,
the more joy you can contain.

—Kahlil Gibran

Our present moment includes the particles we created at that time—not only what actually transpired, but also our subjective view of it. The incidents that make up everything that has ever happened to us, good or bad, move forward and exist in the present by virtue of what we have decided about them. They sit in our energy field, so to speak. They influence us at every moment, whether we are aware of it or not.

—Bearcloud, *7 Fires*

The Inventory

The next steps of the AA program are as follows, and again, with some revisions:

4. I made a searching and fearless moral inventory of my life and myself.

5. I admitted to the Spirit, to myself, and to another human being the exact nature of how I have harmed others and how I have been harmed by others.
6. I am now entirely ready to have the Spirit provide thorough healing for my pain.
7. I humbly ask the Spirit to provide complete and permanent healing in all the areas of my life that are ready for this transformation.

The inventory is taking a long, hard look at what your life has become, as we have begun to do in previous modules. I have made strong attempts to not arouse undue shame, because you may already have enough of that. I have also attempted to redirect focus from what you have "done wrong" to who you really are as a divine being. I am sure this will help a lot in recovery.

I believe that a beneficial inventory will include acknowledging not only all the ways you have made mistakes and hurt others but also how you have been hurt and wounded by others. The word is *trauma*, and the trauma in your life, is the pain and suffering you hold inside and may not have sufficiently processed.

These are the wrongs done to you, which are as important to consider as your wrongs done to others. As the saying goes, "hurt people, hurt people," so it is essential to heal your hurts so you won't keep hurting others.

The process is determining what the wounds of your life are (step 4), how you have hurt others and how others have hurt you. Then being honest about your pain by admitting it to the Spirit, self, and another person (step 5).

Yes, it will be very important to find the right person to admit these important findings to. This is very important, yet it may be difficult to find the right person. I would encourage you to contact me if necessary.

The next steps are to become ready for the Spirit to remove all the hurts and wounds of your life and humbly ask for them to be removed (steps 6 and 7). Once attention and processing are applied to the traumas of your life, it is an inevitable next step for a thorough renovation to occur by the greater power in you.

And by the way, a trauma is something that has occurred in your life that, when it is recalled, arouses any level of emotional response. The emotion that resurfaces when remembered may not be the same as when the event occurred. It is some version of emotional distress, because it remains alive and unprocessed in you.

What may be beneficial here is the ACE, which is a questionnaire that records adverse childhood experiences. Here is an article by NPR that will help you understand the ACE and a link to take the quiz: https://www.npr.org/sections/health-shots/2015/03/02/387007941/take-the-ace-quiz-and-learn-what-it-does-and-doesnt-mean.

Take some time to explore this as we consider your childhood experiences and the pain that may be driving your behaviors.

We will begin now by looking at how you have been wounded. This is an important first step, because how you have been harmed is nearly always the precursor to harming others. It may be impossible for anyone to harm another person, unless they have first been harmed.

The Memory

In this section, we will explore your hurts and wounds, the traumatic occurrences throughout your life. The purpose is the healing of this pain, which has aroused any level of suffering for you.

This will require that you go back to key moments in your life, perhaps in childhood, when these events happened. In doing so, it will be important that you choose a memory that you can recall with some clarity. In other words, a memory that registers a high enough level of distress in the present for you to enter and experience deeply.

The memory or memories you choose are up to you. It can be intense or mild. Only make it strong enough so there is a high capacity for healing. The stronger the emotion in the memory, the more potential there will be to heal.

You do not need to be in the memory as a participant; you can be an observer. You can see it from above, if that is easier. You may rise above as the watcher of this life experience. You can also stop the process at any time if it is too intense.

Take a moment to pick a memory. Recall a life event and begin to view it for what it was and for what it is for you now. Clear away, as much as you are able, all the ways you have added to the picture over the years. I know that is hard, if not impossible.

Simply return to the memory and see it in the way it occurred without editing or altering. Be in this memory, and look around in every way possible. Begin to see what happened for what it was.

Additionally, come into neutrality as much as you can, even with the other players in your memory. The focus is on your healing, and you may need to suspend your hatred and judgment so that these factors do not derail you.

Also, the image may be power-packed with distressing emotions, so let this be. Offer compassion, not judgment, in the best manner possible, as you feel what you need to feel as this memory is brought back to awareness.

Emotions

Regarding your emotional state as you entertain this picture from the past, what is your level of distress? This is to be rated for what it is right now, not when it occurred.

Grade this on a 0–10 scale, with 10 being the most distressing and 0 holding no distress at all. Five is somewhere in between, in the middle. Give it a number on this scale and record it here, ______, or in a notebook.

The Belief

Now we are going to consider what you came to believe about this experience. This may be obvious as thoughts and perceptions arise that you have developed in response. Yet you may want to dig a little deeper, because there is likely a thought behind the thought, a belief beneath the belief that you are most conscious.

This is important because the belief may just be what is keeping this trauma alive over all this time. The event is one factor, and the emotion is yet another, but it is very possible that what you have believed about what happened to you keeps you locked into the event. Yes, it is likely that what you believe about this event is keeping you from healing.

The belief must be recognized, and you must be willing to reformulate it for healing to occur. The beliefs that are most troublesome to us are subconscious, beneath the level of conscious awareness. It will, however, be sufficient for you to record what you are aware of.

If you want to go deeper, there is a list of forty beliefs I developed that may be most beneficial in this process. You may email me, and I will select the belief or beliefs that are most pertinent to this process for you. I will then email what I have found back to you. My email is tomstewardpa@gmail.com.

Central Channel Breathing

An important aspect of this process is breathing. Some very intense emotions may arise, so finding a way to move through them via the breath will be essential.

Imagine there is a channel or a tube in you, just inside the spine. This channel spans the distance from above your head through the body to your core and center in the gut, then down through your torso and legs to the earth below.

For our purposes here, I am asking that you breathe in through your nose on the inhale, down to your belly. This is called abdominal breathing, or the Buddha belly breathing. Then on the exhale, bring your breath back up from the abdomen and out through your nose. Your breath will span the distance from your nose to your belly, down on the inhale and back up on the exhale.

This version of nasal breathing is known as yoga breath, or by the Sanskrit term *pranayama*. We will identify a memory and its associated emotions. You will also find the feeling(s) in your body. The emotion may be in a particular location, like your gut or your heart or throat. You will then breathe in through the nose down to the belly, and then back up on the exhale and out through the nose.

If you are able, maintain some sense of awareness of your breath moving through the area where you sense the tension of the emotion you are feeling. Breathe, down and in, through the area in the body where the emotion is located. (You may want to practice this method of breathing at least for a few breaths before we proceed to the following process.)

And now, take this memory with its corresponding emotions and belief, and begin the following process. (I would encourage you to write about this experience in your journal or a notebook.)

The Process

Memory. Choose a memory in your life, a painful event that has resulted in distress for you. Go into the memory and look around. Be present with this image from the past, allowing yourself to enter in and experience it for what it was.

See it with new eyes, and perhaps, from a different vantage point. What happened? What did another person or others do in this memory? What did you do? How did you respond?

Emotion. What did you feel when that memory occurred? What do you feel about it now? Identify the emotion and put a label or name on that feeling. Also, find this feeling in your body.

Engage in central channel breathing, down and in and through. Breathe through the nose, down to the belly on the inhale, and back up on the exhale and out through the nose.

Stay with this until you feel a shift in you or as long as you feel necessary.

Belief. What did you come to believe about life and yourself in response to the above event? How has this belief helped you to make sense of and process this painful memory? Does this belief currently benefit you or not? Are you willing to let go of this belief, particularly if it stands in the way of your healing?

What is it that you would like to believe instead? How would this new belief change your life and how you live? How would it change you as a person and how you feel? How would it enable you to envision a more hopeful future?

Now, take a few moments to collect yourself. Do some more breathing if you need to. Engage in some version of self-care if you find this necessary.

Processing

This may not have worked for you in the way you expected, and that is okay. You may have felt that this did not go very deep, yet whatever happened is right and good. Whatever you are able to do is just fine.

I know it may take a while to heal the very painful events of your life. Be patient and know you are doing the best you can.

Do you want to know the best and right way to do this? It is what you did, and that is all. Accept that and know that your healing is in *the process*.

In response to this, you may notice shifts and changes in you, or not. You may feel lighter as if something that was present is no longer present. You may have noticed nothing at all, and that is just fine.

This is called processing, and it may take several minutes, several hours, or several days, or longer. When any version of tension or emotional distress arises, return to your central channel breathing. Make deeper breathing a natural part of your life.

You could engage the above steps repeatedly if you like, so return to it again as you are able and willing. You do not need to process all the memories of your life to experience complete healing. One memory at a time will do.

The interesting aspect about memories is that they are held in compartments, much like file folders in a filing cabinet. One memory is cataloged in a file that also has many similar memories. As one memory is processed, many associated memories also heal.

I would encourage you to ask the following questions now, or later when your processing feels more complete.

- What is your new insight and perspective about the memory you have selected?
- What are the new feelings that are beginning to flow in you?
- What is the new belief? What have you chosen to believe as a replacement for the original belief?
- Who do you need to forgive or be forgiven by?

If there is anyone you need to forgive, take note of this, and we will approach this in Module V. For now, let's move on to the next module about how your actions have impacted your relationships.

Module IV

Relationship Repair

We don't see things as they are, we see them as we are.
—The Babylonian Talmud

Emotions

I have often thought that there are two tasks that define our lives. One is to develop skills to manage emotions, and the other is to develop skills to manage relationships. Oddly enough, there is much overlap in this management program.

I would like you to consider your emotions again. We will look at your emotions in a different way in this module. What I aim to highlight are the routine emotions that occur in your life from day to day. Regarding these emotions, what is typically occurring? Who is involved? Who is it that is doing something that arouses an emotional reaction in you?

Additionally, who annoys or frustrates or bothers you the most? If you are prone to anger, what angers you the most? In what situations is your anger aroused? If you often feel hurt or sad, what hurts or saddens you the most? And what about fear—what are you most afraid of, and how does this show up in your life? When and how is anxiety or nervousness or even panic revealed in your life?

Now, I would like to know about the times when any of the above emotional states do not arise in your life. When do you feel like a saint because you are not triggered? Have you noticed times when anger, hurt, sadness, anxiety, fear, nervousness (and the like) do not present themselves? Why do your emotions come up in some situations and not in others?

Familiars

Feelings and emotional states arise, and you get stuck in them because they are familiars. You have had them before. The hurtful emotion that happened in the past, when unresolved, repeats itself. It does this over and over, providing an opportunity to be processed.

If there is a trigger to a previous experience, wouldn't you say that what is occurring is more about your history (what has happened) rather than your present (what is occurring)?

This is how it usually happens. A situation arises, and you are not at all troubled in any way because there is no familiar; there is nothing that is triggered. You go about your business and forget all about it. You may reflect on how you handled that situation well, or maybe not. It is so routine and uneventful you may disregard it rather swiftly.

Then there are other circumstances where your familiar spills out like a flooding torrent. Oops! This includes any of the emotions common to humans. That person, that situation, when *that* happens, it gets you all hot and bothered, and you blame it on the situation at hand or who is present. It must be about what's going on and what the other person did, right? It can't be you; it's *them*. The infamous *they* did it.

It's you, just admit it. LOL! Okay, a better way to say that is you will need to look at your own contribution and reactions if you ever expect your relationships to improve. These situations are opportunities to resolve your familiars.

I often say, if someone pushes your buttons, get rid of your buttons. That's your job. Blaming your distress on the other person while expecting them to change so you don't get triggered isn't the path to peace and harmony. To grow, you need to own your stuff and take care of it by doing your work. It is up to you to remove the triggers of your familiars so you can heal.

Take a Look at Yourself

As we consider these circumstances in this way, there may be little or no reason to blame anyone for the emotions that routinely come up for you. In truth, when an emotion arises, you can say this to the other person: "Hey, I'm feeling _______ right now, and I need to go figure out what this means to me and where it came from. I'll get back to you later. Thanks." That's better than saying, "You make me angry. Because of what you did, I am so _______. I hate you!" You know, stuff like that.

I would strongly suggest that when you have an emotion, know that it is all about you. Resist the urge to blame the other person at all or even the circumstance. There is no person or situation bigger than the old emotions you carry around inside of you. When the emotions arise, they present opportunities for you to do your work.

You had that emotion before the event occurred or before the other person did anything. What is happening and who is involved are simply a way to pop the cork regarding what has been in you for possibly quite some time.

Truthfully, you ought to be grateful for what happened. The other person and the situation are a gift to help you realize where you need emotional healing. You must be ready for this divinely orchestrated event—because it happened.

There is a book I own that I keep on one of my bookshelves. It is entitled *Thank You So Much for Being a Pain.* I have to tell you something about that book. I've never read it. I don't need to; the title says it all.

Have you ever thought of thanking the people who bug the hell out of you? Try it. I would suggest doing that in your own head rather than saying, "Hey, thanks for being a turd muffin. I'm really growing because of you."

More Steps

The next steps in the AA program are these:

8. I made a list of all persons I had harmed and became willing to make amends to them all.
9. I made direct amends to such people wherever possible, except when to do so would injure them or others.
10. I continued to take personal inventory, and when I was wrong, I promptly admitted it.

Now, as you put these steps into action, what is most important is your acknowledgment of harm done. Increasing awareness of how you have behaved, which has hurt others, is important in this process.

You may or may not make directs amends with those you mention. Direct contact may bring additional harm, yet it can also be very healing and liberating for you and the other person. If you have questions about what to do, you can ask another person who has been through this.

Again, this is an ongoing process, and you may work these steps over and over for quite some time. Let's start with the list as suggested in step 8.

Write down the first names or initials of those whom you have harmed. If you write them down in the space below, make sure it is for your eyes only. You may want to use a notebook or journal for privacy.

Okay, what did you do to bring harm to the other person? What was your offense? How did you behave that was hurtful? Write this down here.

Are you willing to make amends to this person? Do you want this relationship to improve? Why or why not? This may not be possible because the person lives far away, or you have no contact with them, or they are deceased. I am asking if you are willing to make amends even if it does not involve the other person. Write about this here in the space below.

I would like to ask that you communicate what you have found here to a trusted person. This cannot be just anyone; it must be someone who knows what to do and, hopefully, has been through it themselves. If you are in therapy, you could tell your therapist, especially if they are familiar with recovery ideals. If you are in a recovery program, you can tell a trusted person who is farther along than you are. Write the name of this person in the space below and mention how you will initiate contact with them.

For step 9, decide whether it would be beneficial to you and the other person or persons to have a discussion with them. This was hopefully considered in the interaction you had with the trusted person above. Only admit your contribution here, not what the other person did.

You would say, "I did ______. I was wrong and I am deeply sorry. Will you forgive me?" In the space below, write down how you will carry this out.

Now, I am going to ask that you make a big change to your life. This is to be so honest with yourself on a day-to-day basis that when the situations described above come up, you would immediately address them or take care of them as soon as you are able.

This is step 10. When you have done something wrong, promptly admit it to yourself first. If it is safe and reasonable to do so, admit your offense to the person you are interacting with. This is your ongoing personal inventory.

Communication 101

When you communicate to someone about anything, really, yet particularly those difficult conversations, there is a procedure I would like to recommend. The words you can offer that can be of help are about what you see, how you feel, and what you need. This includes observation, emotion, and need.

Healthy communication begins with observation, describing the situation. This is the way you observe or observed what is or was occurring. It is what you see or saw.

When you express this, it is best to do it in as neutral terms as possible. Do not say, "When you did that, you made me feel . . ." Eliminate blame and judgment as much as you can or completely. It is as simple as "I see . . ."

Additionally, an important aspect of any communication is expressing how you feel. Your feelings are important, and so are the other person's emotions. Attempt to be as accurate as possible, providing the primary emotion that you feel on a deeper level. You may simply say, "I feel . . ."

Putting those two together, the communication may be expressed in this manner: "When we had that conflict the other night, I said things that I regret. What you said really hurt me and I wanted to let you know." Or "when that happens, I feel hurt, and then anger." You may even add that you are seeking forgiveness for how you expressed your emotions.

I believe the observation and emotion part of the conversation are the most useful. What you need can be added to the other two or it can be offered by itself. Saying "I need . . ." instead of "I want you to . . ." or "You should . . ." is a better option.

So "I see . . . I feel . . . I need . . ." is a helpful way to inform others of your experience on a matter. Give it a try in the way that best suits you and fits your style.

Now, let's go a little deeper into the forgiveness process.

MODULE V

Forgiveness and Amends

Having *"had what are called vital spiritual experiences . . . They appear to be in the nature of huge emotional displacements and rearrangements. Ideas, emotions, and attitudes which were once the guiding forces of the lives of these (individuals) are suddenly cast to one side, and a completely new set of conceptions and motives begin to dominate them."*
—*The Big Book of AA*

Review

Let's review what we have been through so far, which will include looking again at the steps we have covered.

First, there is an admission that you were powerless over alcohol or any behavior and your life had become unmanageable. In so doing, you saw that there is a power from the Source and Spirit that can restore you and heal you. Then you decided to turn your life and will over to the care of this greater power. This is consistent with the way you have understood this advanced Being.

You then engaged in a deep search regarding all the ways you have been harmed and brought harm. This includes your pain and hurt and wounds—the traumas of your life. You were honest with yourself about these events, admitting to the Spirit, to yourself, and to another trusted human being the specifics of these occurrences in your life.

In this admittedly long process, which is ongoing, you became ready to have the Source remove those distressing energies in you. You then humbly ask that these issues of your life be removed.

You considered those individuals you have harmed and were willing to make amends to restore these relationships as much as this is prudent or possible.

You are now in an ongoing program of a daily personal inventory, considering the ways you bring harm or receive harm on a day-to-day basis. In this way, you promptly admit the events that are not becoming of your true nature as a divine being.

Now, let's take a closer look at the forgiveness process.

Forgiveness

Most spiritual traditions wisely assert and practice not bringing harm, even when you have been harmed or not paying back evil when evil was given to you. The best way to retaliate against someone who has brought pain to you is to move from unkindness to kindness, revenge to mercy, and bitterness to forgiveness. This is, admittedly, very difficult to do.

Forgiveness is a way to do important housecleaning in your body/soul system. It is an action that represents many faith traditions yet can also be implemented by those who do not hold to a faith tradition at all. It will be my aim to represent the practice of forgiveness in a way that can be assimilated by anyone and everyone.

In your life, there have been many people who have caused you harm. Scottish poet and lyricist Robert Burns, regarded as the national poet of Scotland, has penned this line: "Man's inhumanity to man makes countless thousands mourn."

Every day of your life, there is one little thing or another, or one big thing or another, that is offered by someone that you may consider offensive or even deeply painful.

There are people in your life, some close to you and some not, who deliver offensive action, which incites any number of emotional experiences. There are circumstances and situations and institutions that may offend you.

There are those moments in your life when you might consider God or the Divine to be the offender, who has delivered harmful action or inaction toward you. Many times, you feel like a victim to the whims of others, who break your heart again and again as the pain strikes deep within.

In response, you always have a choice. You can retain these swirling energies and choose to keep your emotions in you and not forgive. This leads to bitterness and resentment, and the pain of hurt and anger is now turned inward. I have heard it said that this is like swallowing poison, hoping the other person will die. Retaining pain helps no one, and it hurts you the most.

You always have the choice to extend gracious forgiveness to the other person in a way that frees you. This is so liberating, yet it seems to be such a painfully protracted process, one that takes a very long time, perhaps many years to finalize.

There is no hurry with forgiveness, and this long process has a way of foraging a new way in you. No matter how many seasons forgiveness takes, every single moment along the way is important to your growth and recovery.

Forgiveness is the willingness to grant mercy to others, self, and/or God. This can occur even when the offending person is not present. The other person may no longer be living or is somehow inaccessible to you.

To forgive, you don't need the other person; you only need you. Forgiveness is not offered for the other person or with them as the key player. It is for you, because you are the key player. It's your work, a gift to yourself. Forgiveness is a loving action to you.

When you forgive, it does not let the other person off the hook or somehow say their actions are excusable. You forgive for you, and the other person has their own work to do that is separate from yours. Their work is not your business; it is theirs. Your business is to love yourself enough to forgive.

In forgiving, you are not exonerating the other person; in fact, you aren't doing anything at all with the other person. You are simply and exhaustively getting them and the emotions from the event or events out of you.

You are flushing your system of harmful energies, which have been corroding your body and soul for too long. I have been known to say, "Forgive until you hear the flushing sounds."

Forgiving Others

A statement of forgiveness can be as short and simple as the following:

I choose to forgive ________________ for ________________.

This could be presented a few times or many times. You could also say you choose to no longer hold anything against this person and that you release them to the Spirit, letting go of all the harmful energies you have been holding on to.

The idea of revenge or getting back at the one who offended you is so deadly and insidious. You may feel like the other person deserves some sort of retribution for what they did. Or you may feel that this perceived strong response of judgment and hatred somehow protects you. It does no such thing.

To truly forgive, you need to release all these mental machinations. Namely because this is a preoccupation with the other person. Forgiveness happens most swiftly and exhaustively when you lovingly consider yourself and leave the other person to their own path.

An extended version may look like this (you may provide a substitute for God):

> I choose to completely, thoroughly, and permanently forgive _________________ for _________________.

> It is my intention to no longer hold anything against _________________ for his/her actions or inactions.

> As I forgive _________________ once and for all, I also ask God to grant forgiveness to _________________ for what she/he has done or left undone.

> I offer blessing to _________________, and I also ask God to bless _________________.

> I choose to extend love and mercy to _________________, and I ask God to supply love and mercy to _________________.

If you were able to pray that prayer, how did that feel? Did you sense something exit you so that you became lighter? Did you come to know a freedom, as if you were set free from an entanglement that has bound you to your past and what happened? Did you feel more impelled to live from this day forward to a liberated future, instead of being shackled to a past that kept you locked into what occurred? I hope so.

Consider the following statements that could also be offered:

> If there is anyone or anything that has hurt me in the past, knowingly or unknowingly, I forgive and release it.

> If I have hurt anyone or anything in the past, knowingly or unknowingly, I forgive and release it.

> I perform this for the highest good of others and myself.

In addition, visualizing the offending person as their true self, who they really are, may assist you. You could see them with the Divine, who offers merciful kindness toward them.

You could see the Spirit forgiving them and blessing them as you seek to forgive them and bless them. You may see the Source extending love and mercy toward this person as you choose to do the same.

Judgment

When you have been harmed or offended by another person, there is almost always, or perhaps always, judgment that is associated with it.

This may not be hard to comprehend. When someone hurts, there would have to be judgment. The other person did something harmful, and you have judged them. Isn't that a natural response?

I'm not using judgment in any negative manner, particularly at the onset. I am suggesting that judgment tends to grow over time and can, in and of itself, be destructive. It may be what is associated with unforgiveness that results in bitterness.

As judgment evolves, there is the tendency to blame the other person for your unhappiness. If they did not hurt you in the way they did, your life would have been different; you would be happy.

In these situations, you need to not only release unforgiveness but also the judgment associated with it. Forgiving yourself for judging is a powerful action that can be added to this practice.

Unforgiveness and judgment are destructive powers. When you do not forgive, you bring harm to you, at times as intensely as the harm that came from the hands of another. Now you live with double assault. You have been assaulted by someone, and then you bring assaultive action to yourself.

Judgment, in the best sense, is something offered to properly assess the situation. I would only add here that there does come a time when judgment of the other person needs to be suspended. After a certain point, it doesn't serve any purpose.

Judgment can then be reapplied to yourself so you know what you are to do for yourself. The judgment that outlives its usefulness can have negative consequences yet, when used wisely, can be very beneficial.

Seeking Forgiveness

Forgiveness may also include seeking forgiveness from another person. You have not only been harmed, but there are inevitably those times when you have also harmed another person. We have discussed this in other modules, yet I will add a few more thoughts here.

In seeking forgiveness from another person, you can say the following:

> I behaved in the following way ____________ (be specific), and I realize I hurt you. I seek your forgiveness. Will you please forgive me?

You will need to have wisdom and discretion in seeking forgiveness from another person, or you may make matters worse. The above ought to be routine as you seek to take responsibility for every action in your life, even the so-called small ones. This is true, whether you speak to the other person or not.

When there is something much bigger that you have done, and you are reminded of it; you will need to offer reconciliation to do your part to make matters right. This is a tender process, and much guidance is required. I would encourage you to consult with your mentors about this.

Your drinking, or any behavior, could have resulted in any version of violation. This includes emotional and physical and sexual harm. You may be in legal or financial trouble that was harmful to another. You may have been to jail or prison, or you may owe someone money. It is very possible that your actions were quite severe, and you hurt others in critical ways. There may have been inaction on your part, and another person may feel abandoned.

If you do talk to the offended person, you may ask if there is any form of retribution that they require. You will need to use wisdom as you take this into advisement. This doesn't mean you will do anything they ask just because you are the offending party.

I hope this helps. Now, let's move on to the next module—transcendence. This describes how your true self is becoming more evident as you have proceeded through the first ten steps.

Module VI

Transcendence

Most of us struggle with simply being present. Some of us "check out" because we have not confronted our own pain and therefore cannot be present to the pain or demands of others. Others of us are so conditioned to think it is what we do and accomplish that counts that we've never developed a practice of simply being present.
—K. Killian Noe, *Descent into Love: How Recovery Café Came to Be*

Spiritual Practice

The eleventh step of the AA program is as follows (with minor revisions):

> 11. I sought through prayer and meditation to improve my conscious contact with God, Spirit, or Source, as I understood this being, praying only for knowledge of divine will for me and the power to carry that out.

In the above quote by Killian Noe, she offers that we tend to struggle with being present. There may be moments when you check out, you are not present because you have not confronted your own pain.

Evidently, traversing through your life's painful history is a precursor to your transcendence.

It is possible that you have not developed a practice of simply being present, or at least one that is consistent enough to assist in your progression. This, in and of itself, is healing and transformative.

In working through this program, you have begun to confront your pain. You have been courageous in your pursuit to resolve the issues of your life. You have done your work, and you continue to do so.

Pause for a moment and ponder each of the previous modules you have navigated. Consider the work you have finalized and how much you have grown. Take a moment to congratulate yourself for these fine achievements, by you and for you. Excellent work!

Much of your life may have been responding to the fitfulness and turmoil of daily events generated by your own issues and a life of chaos around you. As you begin to resolve these personal dilemmas— healing your hurts and wounds and forgiving yourself and others— there is now an increased opportunity to nurture a spiritual life. Perhaps it is your pain walk that has ushered you into a life of depth and richness.

I will say more about spiritual awakening in the next model, yet for now, let's begin to integrate a certain spiritual practice each day that will result in your transcendence. You have progressed as you heal your pain, and you will progress even more as you enter the blessed sacrament of the present moment.

When Killian writes about the need to develop a spiritual practice of being present, she is referring to the current moment. Everything else—an imagined future and a perceived past—is delusion. They do not exist. They are not real. There is only *now*—the continually unfolding present moment of the *eternal now*.

Some call this eternity, and it surely is. There is a place beyond the limited constructs of time and space, careening more swiftly than the speed of light yet, at the same time, holding a pose of abject stillness in a single now-moment. This is where the spirit of your true self exists in the infinite sense.

You have concluded that you are a body on earth with an ego mind who may have had spiritual experiences in some rare and fleeting moments. Truth is, you are a spiritual being having a human experience for just a short while.

Imagine for a moment your true identity and what a transcendent being you really are. You are as deep and wide and broad as the cosmos, outside of you and inside of you. The vastness of space in all the trillions of solar systems and galaxies throughout known and unknown existence is equal in measure to the infinite dimensions within you. Ponder that.

Your spiritual practice is learning to be present in this now time while accessing the infinite dimensions available to you in any moment. There may be a recognition of a divine being, something beyond you and in you. It may be an experience with your own divinity, your true divine nature.

You may find the invisible attributes of a transcendent essence in nature around you. As you venture into the physical world, you encounter spiritual realities not seen by the naked eye, even though much may be seen with the physical eyes.

There are those simple quiet moments of calm when there is nowhere to go and no one to be, you just are. You are present, captivated by the powerful sway of the subtle rhythms held within a now time-clasp. To arrive at this still point is your spiritual practice, yet as a practice, you must enter this sacred embrace intentionally. You must want the transcendent, to be the transcendent one, as transcendental realities encircle you, resting upon you like a warm blanket.

As often as you are able, I would encourage you to depart from the cacophonous rhythms of the busy life that you may have concluded is so hard to escape. All the tasks before and all the life worries that bombard you in each moment are what you transcend and move beyond. In this way, you enter the present.

Take in a little peace. Breathe, breathe deeply, deeper than you normally do. Choose not to engage the busy as much as this is possible. Find a quiet corner, undistracted by the wildness that life can bring. Wake up early, or stay up late, to avoid the racket, and just be—be in this moment.

Some are able to do this best while in motion—walking and running and dancing—any hallowed movement of the body. When movement enables you to remain present and interiorly calm and centered, you are benefitted.

And then, no matter what is occurring outside of you in the unpredictable fluctuations of life's vicissitudes, present-ness overtakes. Realize that none of the rising cascade of life's assaults need disrupt this inner flow. Descend into your sacred core, slide in, and nothing will lead you away from your own divine center.

Plato's Myth of the Cave

Over thirty years ago, I purchased, possibly accidentally yet fortuitously, a book on philosophy. I never really read much of it, but I scanned through this book on many occasions. As I did, I read the author's interpretation of Plato's allegory of the cave. I was so moved that I have repeated this story to many people over the years.

In this essay, Plato offers a fictional conversation between his two created figures—Socrates and Glaucon. In this tale, there is a cave, dark and musty, with prisoners sitting and facing a wall. Each of these prisoners is fastened at the wrists and ankles and neck. They are not able to move their heads to see anything but the wall before them. They are unable to see anything around them, including themselves. They have been in this state all their lives and know of no other existence.

Behind the prisoners is another shorter wall, and behind this are individuals passing to and fro, carrying objects on their heads. It is here that a fire burns brightly, allowing the reflection of their images and objects to be cast upon the wall in front of the prisoners. The prisoners only hear the muffled voices of those on the other side of the smaller wall. The shadows and echoes are all the reality the prisoners have ever known.

Beyond where these prisoners sit is a passageway, which leads to the outside world. The passage is long enough so no light from the outside can penetrate to be cast upon the prisoners. For these prisoners, it is always dark, always night, and they have never known any comforting light from the other world. Ironically, their freedom, the freedom they do not know exists, is only a short distance away.

There is one prisoner who is somehow released from his confinement. This chosen prisoner is set free from his chains, reportedly with force. He then rises to walk through the passageway to the lighted world outside. At first, the glare of the sun is blinding, yet he eventually becomes accustomed to it as he settles into his new life.

This man, in his freedom, ponders those other prisoners he left behind. He then returns to the cave to tell the others what he has come to know. What he describes to them is unintelligible, and they believe he has lost his mind. They threaten to attack him, if only they could. He finally realizes he is unable to persuade them. The escaped prisoner then returns to the world of light to carry out his new life. His liberation is lost to the prisoners in the cave, and sadly, he leaves them to their chosen confinement.

Coming Out of the Cave

Glaucon's initial response to the telling of Plato's fanciful tale by the myth's character Socrates is as follows: "It's a strange image you're describing, and strange prisoners."

Yet not so strange at all, really, because it hints to the familiar in each one of our lives. We may resemble these prisoners more than we would likely care to admit.

And then, to press further about the ones who dwell imprisoned in the darkness, the figure Socrates in this drama states: "Consider . . . what being released from their bonds and cured of their ignorance would naturally be like." Yes, consider what that would be like for such one to break free—no longer bound—and to see the light, to be enlightened.

In reading through this story, it appears that what Plato hopes to convey is that there is a reality for many that seems so true, for it is all that is known. Even more, there is a wider truth that the unenlightened individual apparently has no conscious awareness until they are awakened.

Imagine life for these prisoners and how it may coincide with your life. The features of this life are of being fastened at every point, in a way that limits movement. There is not a seeing of what is true; their only reality are projections cast upon the canvass of the wall as a shadow play of images.

The only sound that is heard are the echoes of muffled voices reverberating through the cave's unilluminated corridors. The true and the real are not at all apprehended in direct experience. Only darkness is known, and there is no awareness of the light that could be cast upon a countenance in dire need of such illumination.

Somehow, in some way, there is one who is allowed to break free. Yet for him, his fate seems to be in the hands of another, as Plato offers, who drags him out of the only life he has ever known.

Interestingly, if there was no force, no other to stimulate movement, there would be no consciousness of the journey of liberation. This one is then released from the bonds and fetters of a limited existence to move through the passageway to the lighted world outside.

Once outside in the light, he looks around and is baffled by the peculiar experience of it all. All is unfamiliar and even uncomfortable, so foreign to what has been previously known. As he adapts to this world of light, he realizes he has discovered a radiant new world, one that holds more depth and meaning. The life he had before was so unidimensional, and now there is so much more to comprehend.

Plato goes on to reason that "the visible realm should be likened to the prison dwelling, and the light of the fire inside it to the power of the sun. And if you interpret the upward journey and the study of things above as the upward journey of the soul to the intelligible realm, you'll grasp what I hope to convey."

There are two realms, at least. There is the realm of the visible, postmarked by the shadow play of images, and the muzzled echoes caroming off the walls in the abject darkness. Perhaps most of us, for most of our lives, live here, not knowing anything else.

There is also the realm of the *beyond* known only by those who have been enlightened, who have seen the light outside the darkened cave. There may be, interestingly, some long line of progression from the first reality to the second world, from the darkened spheres to the lighted realms.

From this allegory, we find through Plato's musings that the progress of the soul is defined by freedom and enlightenment to break free and to see anew what was not before known. This myth from Plato begs us to ask these questions:

What is your reality and what holds your gaze and attention from day to day?

Are there ways in your life that you feel bound and trapped like a prisoner who has very little awareness of how to break free?

What are you seeing, and is it the true and the real or a shadow play of appearances in the darkness?

What are you not seeing, what are you missing because you are confined by your limited perception?

Is what you are apprehending in your life a direct experience of what is most true and real, or are you borrowing from someone else's reality regarding what they told you?

What is the story you live by and what do you keep repeating about yourself and your life?

Have you ever imagined that there is another way to see beyond what you typically perceive?

The Light of Transcendence

Your transcendence consists of leaving your position of entrapment and entering into the light. Initiating a spiritual practice is what will enable you to transcend a limited life like those prisoners in the cave, and then enter the lighted world outside.

In AA, this is referred to as a vital spiritual experience. This is something that happens in certain moments, yet as you progress on the spiritual path, it occurs with more regularity and increased frequency.

Of all the practices you are aware of, which spiritual practice would you like to add to your daily routine? Name just one activity, or two, and perhaps more that you can assimilate into your daily life that will assist you in your transcendence. Write this in the space below.

If nothing else, resolve to enter *the quiet*. There is a place of stillness—it is within you—known most poignantly when you realize there is nowhere to go and nothing to do. There is nothing but being, to be, simply as you are.

It is here that you are present, in the precious now time. In this place, you sense and feel and know your transcendence. You transcend ordinary reality, the life of hustle and grind you have been living, yet you now enter the sublime presentness of eternity.

Now, let's move on to consider this new life you are living in response to your awakening.

MODULE VII

A New Life

*A new life has been given to us or, if you prefer,
'a design for living' that really works.*

—*The Big Book of AA*

Spiritual Awakening

The last step of AA is as follows:

> 12. Having had a spiritual awakening as the result of these steps,
> we tried to carry this message to others, and to practice these
> principles in all our affairs.

To have a spiritual awakening is to wake up, as if from a deep sleep,
a slumber in which eyes are not open or not wide open enough to see
reality as it is. In the awakening, you now see as never before, and
life takes on a renewed perspective.

In what ways do you believe this has occurred to you? How have you awakened as a part of this course as you have completed all the previous modules? Write about this here.

The Awakening Prayer

There is a prayer I developed that I would like to introduce to you. It is called the Awakening Prayer. It comes from a particular passage of scripture in the New Testament, in the letter to the church at Ephesus known as Paul's letter to the Ephesians. The passage is often rendered in this way:

> Awake sleeper, and arise from the dead, and Christ
> will shine on you. (Ephesians 5:14)

I have taken some liberties with the text and have altered it for my purposes as seen below. It also takes into consideration that in your true nature, you already are an enlightened being. You only need to realize this as you become more aligned with your true and higher self.

Christ said that he is the light of the world, yet he also offered that you are the light of the world (John 8:12 and Matthew 5:14). You are a being of light from a domain of brilliant light. Your status as a light being is your true essence that does not need to be achieved for some future time. It is evident now in the inner dimensions of your being. This is what you awaken.

I have prayed the following "Awakening Prayer" over many people, and significant shifts have been noted in every recipient. I am including this prayer here, yet it may be most powerful when done in a group or if someone prays it over you.

If you contact me, I will offer you a session that includes the praying of this prayer. For now, I will include the prayer for you to discern how to use it. (In the first line, enter your name or the recipient's name and the issue to be worked on.)

A prayer on behalf of ________________ regarding ____________________.

Awake sleeper, arise from your slumber, and Christ will radiate light to you, the light that you are.

Christ is the light in the infinite realms. You are the light in the infinite realms.

The one, the invisible spirit, the savior, the figure with several forms within the light, beholding itself in the light, who gives immeasurable and incomprehensible light, speaks to you.

"Let whoever hears this arise from deep sleep."

Wake up! Remember! Awaken to knowledge and salvation. Allow enlightened insight to appear as light to remove the veil that covers the mind so that the mind would be awakened.

Christ heals you. Receive your healing. Be healed.

In your awakening, be the light that you are. And ascend to the perfect realm.

Pray this prayer until you sense it is complete, preferably with the use of a pendulum or some version of intuitive sensing. I usually pray it anywhere from three times up to fifteen times until I sense completion.

After you discern the prayer is complete, say this:

> You are awakened. You are enlightened. The veil over the mind has been removed. You are healed. You have been raised from the deep and sealed in luminous water with five seals. You have ascended.

> (Confirm completion with a pendulum or intuition.)

True Spirituality

I am one who has been on a search for a very long time for authentic spiritual encounter. My objective has been to engage an experience that would facilitate the evolution of my soul and then share the same with others.

I have also considered history and how many spiritual groups were initiated. What I have found is that the original intent of many spiritual groups, if not all, held a simple intention. This was to be a group of spiritual seekers who came to know the Divine Spirit in the deepest and most profound sense.

This is also true for Christianity. In my estimation, what we now know as the Christian religion is something that has veered far off the course of the original intent.

I have been very intrigued by a group of seekers known as the Essenes, who lived in and around the first century. An alternate version of history reveals that this is the group that prepared the way for the teacher of righteousness. This was the man known as Jesus Christ. He was from this group and lived among them during his formative years.

We now know more of what this group of Essenes believed and practiced because of a certain discovery. In 1945, a certain man stumbled upon scrolls of writings that we now know as the Nag Hammadi scriptures. You may have heard of these documents by another name, the Dead Sea Scrolls.

These unearthed scriptures contain many documents that shed new light on the beginnings of Christianity. These books, however, were shunned and disregarded by the ruling hierarchy that resolved to keep the masses in fear and shame. The Nag Hammadi scriptures offer something of a deeper spirituality and a recognition of the radiant beauty within each human. This is not something early church leaders hoped to convey.

One book found in that cave in Upper Egypt is a document known as the *Secret Book of John*. This writing is a conversation between Christ and his dear friend John. The above prayer, the "Awakening Prayer," is gleaned from this document.

I offer this prayer to you for our purpose here. It is meant to direct you into an awakening as you may have never known. I hope this prayer guides your entrance into a new life in ways that benefit you and your recovery.

Waking Up

In response to this program, and/or the prayer above, in what ways have you detected an awakening in you and in your life? What shifts and changes have occurred recently and over time that are like waking up from a deep slumber? Write about this in the space below.

Congratulations! You have officially completed *The Process* and all seven modules of this program. Well done!

Now, do something nice for yourself and let the feelings of accomplishment linger in you for as long as you are able.

Conclusion

Summary of This Program

You have moved through the following modules in this program—*The Process.*

Module 1: *Transparency*
You looked honestly at yourself and your drinking or any troublesome behavior.

Module II: *The Life You Now Live*
You considered the impact of your actions in your life.

Module III: *Sorrows That Carve Deep*
You processed your pain and trauma for healing.

Module IV: *Relationship Repair*
You initiated the process of examining and repairing your relationships.

Module V: *Forgiveness and Amends*
You enacted the actions of forgiving and being forgiven.

Module VI: *Transcendence*
You experienced a spiritual awakening.

Module VII: *A New Life*
You have begun living a new life in response to your awakening.

I would encourage you to return to these modules again and again for the rest of your life and as often as you need to. For now, I would like you to reminisce on one or two takeaways from this program.

What did you learn? What have you been able to integrate into your life? What has helped you the most? Write your answers here.

I am grateful that you have chosen to be a part of this program. I am proud of you for all the work you have done so far and will continue to do. I hope the best for you in this ongoing adventure of the life you have been given.

If you have any need to contact me, please do so at any of these contact information:

+1 505-412-0010
tomstewardpa@gmail.com
www.tomsteward.com
Love and light to you.

Further Reading

1. *The Big Book* of Alcoholics Anonymous
2. *In the Realm of Hungry Ghosts: Close Encounters with Addiction* by Gabor Mate, MD
3. *This Naked Mind: Control Alcohol, Find Freedom, Discover Happiness, and Change Your Life* by Annie Grace
4. *The Energy Codes: The 7-Step System to Awaken Your Spirit, Heal Your Body, and Live Your Best Life* by Dr. Sue Morter
5. *Breaking the Habit of Being Yourself: How to Lose Your Mind and Create a New One* by Dr. Joe Dispenza
6. *Becoming Supernatural: How Common People Are Doing the Uncommon* by Dr. Joe Dispenza
7. *Holy Pride and Love of Self: The Untimely Death of a Son and the Unanticipated Revelation of Heaven* by Tom Steward and Ryan Bradlee Steward
8. *Spirit Code: The Healing of Energies in the Body's Subconscious* by Tom Steward
9. *Loving What Is: Four Questions That Can Change Your Life* by Byron Katie
10. *Descent Into Love: How Recovery Café Came to Be* by K. Killian Noe
11. *7 Fires* by Bearcloud
12. *Divine Therapy & Addiction: Centering Prayer and the Twelve Steps* by Father Thomas Keating

13. *Addiction and Grace: Love and Spirituality in the Healing of Addictions* by Gerald May
14. *The Story of Thought: The Essential Guide to the History of Western Philosophy* by Bryan Magee
15. *The Nag Hammadi Scriptures: The Revised and Expanded Translation of Sacred Gnostic Texts* edited by Marvin Meyer
16. *The Essenes: Children of the Light* by Stuart Wilson and Joanna Prentis
17. *The Gnostic Gospels: Long Buried and Suppressed, The Gnostic Gospels Contain the Secret Writings Attributed to the Followers of Jesus* by Elaine Pagels

9 781669 839286